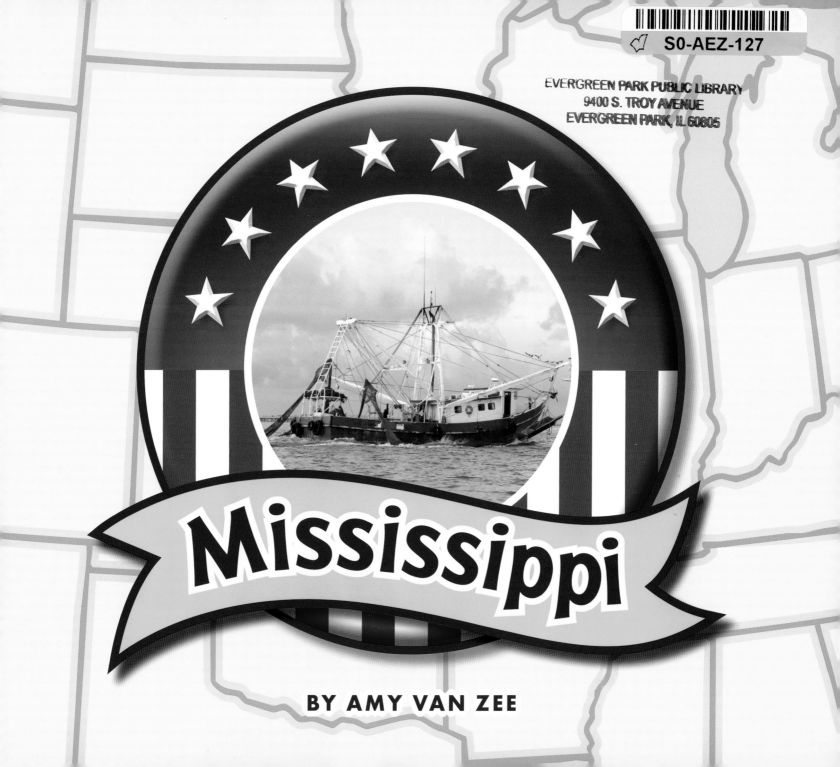

Mississippi

BY AMY VAN ZEE

The Child's World

Published by The Child's World®
1980 Lookout Drive • Mankato, MN 56003-1705
800-599-READ • www.childsworld.com

ACKNOWLEDGMENTS
The Child's World®: Mary Berendes, Publishing Director
The Design Lab: Design and production
Red Line Editorial: Editorial direction

PHOTO CREDITS: Kathy Hicks/iStockphoto, cover, 1, 3; Matt Kania/Map
Hero, Inc., 4, 5; Clyde H. Smith/Peter Arnold Images/Photolibrary, 7;
iStockphoto, 9, 10, 11; Blair Howard/iStockphoto, 13; North Wind Picture
Archives/Photolibrary, 15; Michelle Junior/iStockphoto, 17; Kiichiro Sato/AP
Images, 19; Gordon Ball/iStockphoto, 21; One Mile Up, 22; Quarter-dollar
coin image from the United States Mint, 22

LIBRARY OF CONGRESS CATALOGING-IN-PUBLICATION DATA
Van Zee, Amy.
  Mississippi / by Amy Van Zee.
     p. cm.
  Includes bibliographical references and index.
  ISBN 978-1-60253-468-1 (library bound : alk. paper)
  1. Mississippi—Juvenile literature. I. Title.

F341.3.V36 2010
976.2—dc22

                            2010017926

Printed in the United States of America in Mankato, Minnesota.
July 2010
F11538

On the cover:
Many people
in Mississippi
fish for shrimp.

CONTENTS

Geography

Let's explore Mississippi! Mississippi is in the southern United States. The **Gulf** of Mexico is to the south of the state. The Mississippi River is most of Mississippi's western border.

TENNESSEE

Corinth •

• Oxford   • Tupelo

Clarksdale •

ARKANSAS   ALABAMA

Mississippi River

Columbus •

Greenwood •

• Greenville

MISSISSIPPI

Meridian •

Vicksburg • Vicksburg
National
Military Park   ★ **Jackson**

• Natchez

• Hattiesburg

NORTH
WEST   EAST
SOUTH

LOUISIANA   FLORIDA

Bay
Saint   Gulfport
Louis   • Biloxi

5

Gulf of Mexico

Cities

Jackson is the capital of Mississippi. It is also the largest city in the state. Gulfport, Biloxi, Hattiesburg, and Greenville are other large cities.

About 150,000 people live in Jackson. ▶

Land

The land around the Mississippi River is good for farming. The state has many rolling hills. Mississippi also has **bayous**.

Trees grow in some of Mississippi's bayous. ▶

Plants and Animals

Forests cover more than half of Mississippi. The magnolia tree grows throughout the state. The tree's **petals** are large and white. The magnolia is both the state tree and the state flower. Mississippi's state bird is the mockingbird. Mockingbirds can copy the sounds of other birds.

The magnolia became the Mississippi state flower in 1952. ▶

People and Work

Almost 3 million people live in Mississippi. Many farmers in the state grow cotton. **Manufacturing** is also important in Mississippi. Cars and furniture are made here. Many people work in banks, hotels, and restaurants.

Cattle and chickens are raised in Mississippi.

A machine picks the cotton from a field in Mississippi. ▶

History

Native Americans have lived in this area for thousands of years. The first explorers from Europe came to the area in the 1500s. Mississippi became the twentieth state on December 10, 1817. People from Mississippi fought for the South during the U.S. **Civil War**.

In the 1800s, settlers came to Mississippi in covered wagons. ▶

Ways of Life

Blues, a type of music, is enjoyed in Mississippi. Visitors come to the state for its beaches and sunny weather. The Biloxi Shrimp **Festival** celebrates the start of the shrimp-fishing season. Some people in Mississippi celebrate Mardi Gras. They wear colorful masks and watch **parades**.

The guitar is often played in blues music. ▶

Famous People

Writer William Faulkner was born in Mississippi. Musician B. B. King, singer Jimmy Buffett, and football player Brett Favre are from Mississippi. Jim Henson was born and grew up in the state. He created the Muppets, which are a group of puppets. Singer Elvis Presley was born in Mississippi. Oprah Winfrey was born in the state, too.

Oprah Winfrey has hosted *The Oprah Winfrey Show* since 1985. ▶

Famous Places

Mississippi has many old **plantations**. The Delta Blues **Museum** shows the history of blues music. The Vicksburg National **Military** Park is the location of a famous Civil War battle. Visitors to Mississippi can also see where Elvis Presley was born.

Each year, many people visit the birthplace of Elvis Presley in Tupelo, Mississippi. Presley was born here in 1935. ▶

State Symbols

Seal

Mississippi's state seal shows an eagle. It holds arrows and an olive branch. These stand for war and peace. Go to childsworld.com/links for a link to Mississippi's state Web site, where you can get a firsthand look at the state seal.

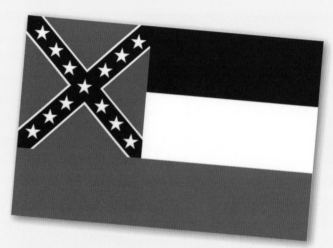

Flag

Mississippi's state flag was adopted in 1894. It has a **Confederate** flag in the upper left corner.

Quarter

The Mississippi state quarter shows a magnolia, which is the state flower. The quarter came out in 2002.

Glossary

bayous (BYE-ooz): Bayous are swampy and slow-moving bodies of water. Mississippi has bayous.

blues (BLOOZ): Blues is a type of jazz music that is usually slow and sad. Blues is popular in Mississippi.

Civil War (SIV-il WOR): In the United States, the Civil War was a war fought between the Northern and the Southern states from 1861 to 1865. Mississippi fought for the South during the Civil War.

Confederate (kun-FED-ur-it): Confederate refers to something that was a part of the Confederate States of America during the Civil War. Mississippi's state flag has the Confederate flag in the corner.

festival (FESS-tih-vul): A festival is a celebration for an event or holiday. The Biloxi Shrimp Festival is held each year in Mississippi.

gulf (GULF): A gulf is a large body of water with land around most of it. Mississippi is next to the Gulf of Mexico.

manufacturing (man-yuh-FAK-chur-ing): Manufacturing is the task of making items with machines. Some people in Mississippi work in manufacturing.

military (MIL-uh-tayr-ee): The military is the armed forces of a country. The Vicksburg National Military Park is in Mississippi.

museum (myoo-ZEE-um): A museum is a place where people go to see art, history, or science displays. The Delta Blues Museum in Mississippi shows the history of blues.

parades (puh-RAYDZ): Parades are when people march to honor holidays. People in Mississippi watch parades during Mardi Gras.

petals (PET-ulz): Petals are the colorful parts of a flower. The magnolia, Mississippi's state flower, has white petals.

plantations (plan-TAY-shunz): Plantations are large farms where crops are grown. Mississippi has many old plantations.

seal (SEEL): A seal is a symbol a state uses for government business. An eagle is on the Mississippi state seal.

symbols (SIM-bulz): Symbols are pictures or things that stand for something else. The seal and the flag are Mississippi's symbols.

Further Information

Books

Bauer, Marion Dane. *The Mighty Mississippi*. New York: Aladdin, 2007.

Shoulders, Michael. *M is for Magnolia: A Mississippi Alphabet*. Chelsea, MI: Sleeping Bear Press, 2003.

Trueit, Trudi Strain. *Mississippi*. New York: Children's Press, 2007.

Web Sites

Visit our Web site for links about Mississippi: *childsworld.com/links*

Note to Parents, Teachers, and Librarians: We routinely verify our Web links to make sure they are safe and active sites. So encourage your readers to check them out!

Index